FLOWER ARRANGING
BY NUMBER

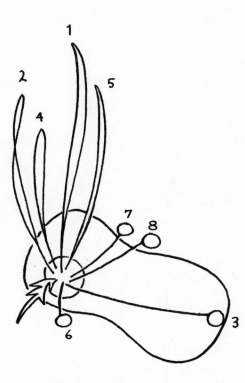

FLOWER ARRANGING
by
number

By

PEGGY BOEHM and SHIZU MATSUDA

Illustrated by S. MATSUDA

GRAMERCY PUBLISHING COMPANY   New York

Acknowledgment
The publishers wish to thank John Yakata
who photographed the flower arrangement pictured on the jacket.

CONTENTS

Introduction

People think you have to be "born" to paint, or act, or arrange flowers, but that isn't true. You can learn to do creative things, even though you may not be richly endowed with creative instincts. It is true that some people are so artistically gifted that they are impelled to write or paint, and do it well even without any training. Nevertheless, everyone is potentially creative. With clear instructions and practice, you can become truly professional at arranging flowers.

Have you ever noticed how easy a thing looks when an expert does it? There's no waste motion, no agonizing period of indecision, no "fuss and feathers." Actually, it's the making of decisions that's the hard part of anything. "Should I add rosemary or marjoram?" "Did I 'ease in' the shoulder seam enough?" "Should the jonquils or the peonies go in front?" "How long should I cut the stems?"

But once you have clear-cut, well-organized, unequivocal directions written in terms you can thoroughly understand, arranging flowers is child's play. And to give such instructions is the aim of this book. The directions and illustrations which follow are so simple you can't miss. You will be able to make arrangements which will hold their own with those produced by the garden-club gals.

It is not our intention, necessarily, to make you a flower arranger. It *is* our intention to teach you how to make a few basic arrangements, and to make them well. Which ones you choose will be up to you. For example, what do you own in the way of "containers?" (Don't let that word throw you—in garden club jargon, it simply means a vase, bowl or pot of some kind to hold water for the flowers.) Where, in your home, do you particularly want flowers? You may be interested primarily in centerpieces for your dining table, or you may like the idea of always having an attractive arrangement on the grand piano or the foyer table, or on great-aunt Lilith's little French secretary between the front windows.

But here's the beautiful part. Once you have any one arrangement down pat, you can make half-a-dozen, even more, without learning anything new! We show you how to vary the essential arrangement according to the season of the year, the color scheme you desire, the formality or informality of the occasion, and in some cases, how to utilize wild flowers and weeds! Even if you learn to master just one basic arrangement, you can use it with infinite variety. However, once you find how easy, satisfying and successful it is to arrange by number, you will want to learn several different designs.

To begin with, you will probably work with the book open in front of you, like a cook trying a new recipe. Where you go from there will be up to you. Soon you may find yourself constructing the basic arrangement from memory, or with only an occasional reference to the book. And then—who knows? Once your fingers have learned the way, you may find them doing strange and wonderful things, almost without any conscious direction from your brain. Your essential creative instinct—and never doubt for a moment that you have one—will find that the path to self-expression is suddenly wide open!

The third part of our book (Idea Section) is especially designed to prod and push and tempt your creative instinct, be it large or small, to think of flower arranging in terms of your home and its furnishings. It is the Idea Section which will spark your imagination. "I don't have a ruby glass goblet," you may say to yourself, "but I have that odd green one left that I couldn't bear to throw away. Why don't I use that instead?" Well, now you're thinking creatively.

Possibly one of the things that interests you particularly is that successful arrangements seem to take so few flowers. You need quite a bunch to make an attractive display when you simply thrust them in a vase. Here you will find ideas galore for taking just a few flowers—really, what you *can* do with three marigolds!—and teaming them up with a bit of bric-a-brac, perhaps Junior's old eggcup, for charming and unusual effects.

"It looks so easy when someone *else* does it" you say? Well, it *is* easy! You can do it too! Here's how.

FLOWER ARRANGING
BY NUMBER

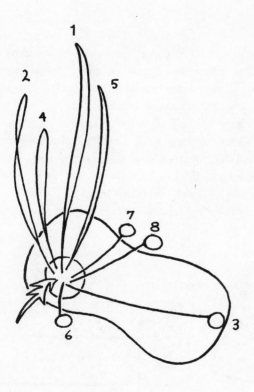

1. You Never Had It So Easy

There are so many bewildering gadgets you can buy nowadays for flower arranging that you will surely welcome our advice. Forget gadgets! You'll need a few frogs or pin holders and some florist's clay—devices to hold your materials in place. That's about the size of it!

Pictured here are some of the holders you may want to buy.

Foam blocks of "Oasis" for fresh flowers and "styrofoam" for artificial flowers make arrangements extra easy to assemble and keep. Cut the styrofoam to fit your container, but let it extend above the rim for ease of inserting stems at any desired angle. Although green styrofoam is not unsightly, you can cover it with sheet moss (available from your florist) for a truly professional touch.

Foam blocks
Good for artificial flowers or emergencies

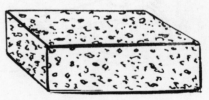

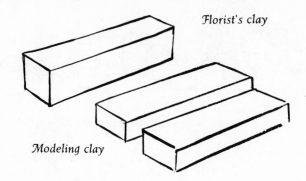

Florist's clay

Modeling clay

Round pin holder

Cup holder with built-in pins

Square pin holder

Oval pin holder

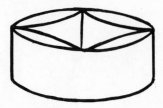

Divided cup holder

Snake holder with built-in pins

Wire holder

CONTAINERS

Now, don't tell anyone we said so, but forget about containers as well as gadgets. If you have any garden club gal friends, you will know instantly that this is even ranker heresy than our first piece of advice. The garden-club gals are constantly prowling through antique shops and thrift shops looking for suitable or unusual or amusing containers. The fact is, if they prowled through *your* house, they would find any number of possible containers. And so will you. Anything that holds water is a container—a layer-cake tin, a big square glass ash tray from the five and

Ash tray arrangement

dime, a shapely bottle which once contained shampoo guaranteed to make you a lovelier you. True, if you want the tall arrangement in a tall vase,

15

Shampoo bottle arrangement

pictured on page 34, you can't make it in a low bowl. You may use an umbrella stand instead of a vase; you may take a tall fruit-juice can and make it appear even taller by tying a flexible split-bamboo table mat around it. If you don't have a tall vase, you may think up an even more ingenious container than a fruit-juice can, but, of course, you can't make this arrangement in a pie plate.

However, if you want flowers for your dinner table or a low coffee table, you can choose an arrangement for which the container is unimportant. A little scrounging through kitchen cupboards or toy chests will uncover a bowl, a box or some object of suitable shape, and if you add some extra greenery at the base of the arrangement, you'll hide the humble container. What if you do have a handsome bowl similar in size and shape to the fluted milk glass bowl illustrated on page 26? So much the better!

Your home is undoubtedly a treasure trove of containers—aside from the orthodox vases and bowls which you already know about—but you really don't have to search for buried treasure. Starting a flower arrangement with the container and working outward from there is only one way to begin. There are several other good methods. However, you will probably want to purchase a few containers, and there are some arrangements for which a specific type of container is vital. Besides, when you get right down to it, "antiquing" is fun!

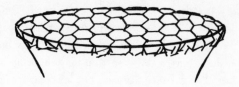

Wide-mouthed container with chicken wire

Wide-Mouthed Containers

Wide-mouthed vases, especially tall ones which are suitable for tall, heavy flowers or branches, present a problem. You have probably discovered this if you have so much as stuck a bunch of lilacs into a jar. The stems won't stay put! We show you how to solve this problem simply and immediately. If you intend to use a tall, wide-mouthed vase, it will be worth your while to buy a very small amount of chicken wire at the hardware store. Cut a piece an inch or two larger in diameter than the mouth of the vase. Center this over the opening, bend down the edges of the wire as tightly as possible and, if necessary, tape the wire into place. Many bowls also take kindly to chicken wire.

Another way to keep flowers in place in a wide-mouthed container is to crisscross the mouth of the vase with strips of sticky cellophane tape. This is a handy makeshift method—provided you can find your roll of cellophane tape!

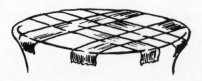

Wide-mouthed container with cellophane tape crisscross

Instant Containers

If you have bowls or other containers which you intend to use frequently, keep them in a state of permanent readiness by anchoring the pin holders or frogs into position as shown below, and simply leave them there. Of course, this means that you'll need to buy several pin holders or frogs, but we told you you'd have to have a good supply, didn't we?

Anchoring holder into place

If we have kept to a minimum the gadgets or containers we suggested for purchase, we hope to approach the maximum in hints and suggestions to make your flower-arranging life a cinch and a pleasure.

WHERE

The first question to ask yourself before choosing an arrangement is where you want to put it. This will save you from making a beautiful arrangement and then wandering around the house, spilling a trail of water — and maybe even flowers — over your rugs as you try it out on the mantel, the buffet and the coffee table. (If you get caught in this dilemma despite our warning, at least make it a "dry run"; add the water *after* your arrangement comes to its final resting place!)

HOW TO BEGIN

Let's say you have decided that the arrangement on page 60 would be just right for the chest of drawers in your entrance hall. You have an appropriate container—a basket with a large handle—and the arrangement itself looks interesting: dark magnolia leaves against a white wall. True, your walls aren't white, but if you read further, you will discover a variation done with autumn leaves. Perfect! The leaves will go well with your cocoa walls. In fact, the variation is super-perfect, for it's autumn, and the leaves are free for the picking. The autumn-leaf group is an excellent choice for a beginner. Next time you can splurge, and do the same arrangement with orchids.

So much for getting started—it's as simple as that!

KEEPING FLOWERS FRESH

Shrubs and flowers with woody stems will last longer if they can absorb quite a lot of water. In order to ensure that they get as much water as possible, use your clippers or a knife to slit the stems up from the bottom about an inch. Make crisscross cuts as indicated in the drawing below. Flowers with stiff stems, like roses, should be cut at an angle so

Crisscross cutting

that the largest possible cut surface will be exposed to the water. (See below.)

Flower life can be prolonged if you cut stems under water and change the water daily. Thick stems should be cut at an angle.

Keep flowers plunged up to their heads in water until you are ready to arrange them. Always arrange them a bit ahead of the time you will need them (this holds especially true for table arrangements), so they will have time to perk up.

Important Hint: Always cut off all leaves which would otherwise be under water. This will keep the water from getting foul as the leaves decay.

ARRANGING FINE-STEMMED FLOWERS

Some flowers have stems too fine to be impaled on the nails of a pin holder. You can easily remedy this by wrapping the stems in $\frac{1}{2}''$ or $\frac{3}{4}''$ squares of paper, as shown below. Then you can squeeze the wrapped stems down between the needles of a pin holder.

Wrap fine stems with paper before inserting pins

HOW TO SHAPE BRANCHES AND STEMS

If you have unlimited bushes to choose from, or flowers, you should theoretically be able to find exactly the sizes and shapes you need. However, most of us have to take what we can get, so to speak; nature doesn't always oblige. However, bending and shaping branches is easier than you may think, and with just a little practice you should be able to do a professional job of it.

All you really need is plenty of water, for you will work under water. But don't run out and buy an aqualung. Only the branches or flowers and your hands will be under the surface.

For soaking branches, use a bucket, your kitchen sink, bathtub, or even a plastic wastebasket. Allow the branch to soak for a few minutes and then, working under water, shape it a little bit at a time with a controlled gentle pressure until you achieve the shape you desire. As the twig is bent, so goes the arrangement!

To shape flower stems, follow the drawing below. You use exactly

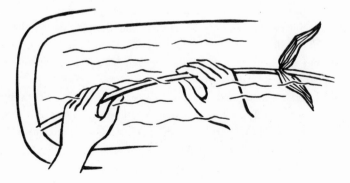

Bending stems under water

the same method as for branches, but stroke the stems even more gently as you work. In some cases, the weight of the bloom alone will cause the stem to bend or sway sufficiently for the effect you want. In fact, sometimes your problem may be how to acquire an erect stem.

HOW TO HOLD FLOWERS ERECT

Occasionally you will find it necessary to prop up a droopy flower, and you can accomplish this easily if you have a small supply of florist's wire on hand. This wire is covered with green paper. Surprisingly, sometimes you can obtain it from a bunch of broccoli! Simply wire the weak-spined stem to another stiffer stem, and it will maintain its posture.

FOOL YOUR PUBLIC

If you're using artificial flowers, follow all the instructions under each arrangement as if you were using fresh. The only difference may be your choice of holders or frogs, since you cannot usually impale the stem of an artificial flower on a pin-holder. Plastic foam blocks are easiest to handle, but for deep containers the chicken wire and cellophane tape methods are just as satisfactory.

And here's a mad, mad idea that makes lots of good sense. Combine fresh and artificial flowers in the same arrangement! The fresh flowers will give even more authenticity to the fake, while the artificial will cut down the cost of your arrangement!

2. Basic Arrangements

AN ALL-POINTS ARRANGEMENT FOR ROUND
OR SQUARE DINNER TABLES

An arrangement used as a centerpiece must be pleasing from all sides, as well as from above. Such an arrangement is suitable for a dining table, a coffee table, a low occasional table or any surface below eye level.

The colorful and festive arrangement pictured in Ill. 1 is for special occasions and it is so extremely simple to arrange, you can treat your family like "company" any night of the week! The bowl in the illustration is fluted milk glass, about 6½ inches in diameter, and the flowers are red tulips, purple hyacinths and lilies of the valley. Their deep, brilliant colors set off a white dinner service and linens to great advantage, and in combination with pastel-colored linens or dinnerware, give a lovely springtime feeling.

For convenience sake in our step-by-step, arranging-by-number directions, we speak of a "front" to the arrangement. Actually, there is no

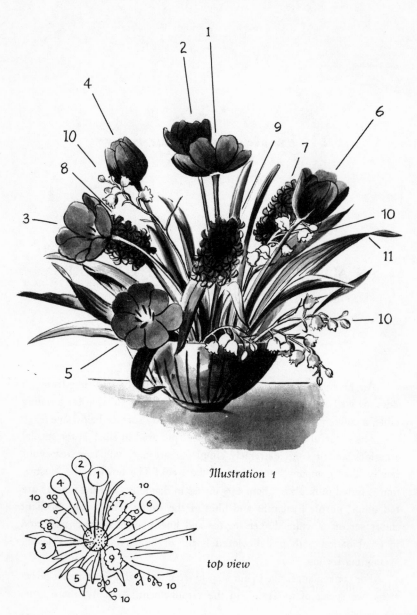

Illustration 1

top view

front. However, when you're finished, you may find that one aspect of the arrangement is more satisfactory than the others, or one particular bloom the most beautiful, and you may want to let that side face the door through which family and friends will enter the dining room.

Before you assemble your floral materials, anchor a pin holder firmly into place in your bowl, using florist's clay as shown on page 19. You will find it best to add the water last, after the arrangement is in place on the table, particularly if the container is quite shallow.

Read through the following steps competely before you begin. Once your materials are assembled and each stalk cut to the required length, the directions plus the aerial diagram serve as a complete guide to making the arrangement.

Materials

6 red tulips
3 purple hyacinths
4 sprays of lily of the valley
leaves cut off of tulips for filler.

If you intend to use an unglamorous container, ask your florist for extra fern or other leaves, or cut sprigs of ilex, taxis, hemlock, laurel or whatever your garden affords in the way of greenery.

All the flowers are numbered. The tulips in this master arrangement, for example, are numbered (1) through (6) in the step-by-step directions as well as in the diagram. Some are full-blown, you will notice, some partly open and some are buds. The directions tell you which are which.

To obtain the appearance of full-blown tulips, gently fold back the petals under water, as shown on the next page. You can do this with roses and other flowers, too.

Where the arrangement calls for a flower to be bent, choose one with an appropriately curved stem if possible. However, if nature does not oblige, you may have to help her along. To bend the stem to a desired shape, follow the directions on page 23.

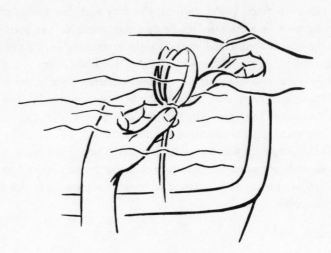

Opening petals under water

Arranging-By-Number, Step-By-Step

Red Tulips

(1): Take a full-blown tulip (1) and cut the stem with a sharp knife to a height of 8¼ inches over-all. Place upright in center, according to the diagram.

(2): Take a partly opened tulip (2) and cut it to a height of 9 inches. Insert it behind and to left of (1), and bend it gently away from the bowl.

(3): Cut a full-blown tulip (3) to 7 inches tall. Place it in front and to the left of (2), bending it outward to the left front.

(4): Cut a tulip bud (4) 9 inches tall and place it between (2) and (3).

(5) : Place a full-blown tulip 5 inches tall in front of (2), and bend it down gently until it is level with the rim of the bowl.

(6) : Take another bud (6) and cut it to 5 inches high. Place it to the right of (1).

Purple Hyacinths

(7) : Cut hyacinth (7) to an over-all height of 7 inches and place it between (1) and (6).

(8) : Place a 7-inch hyacinth (8) between (3) and (4), bending it gently down until it is suspended slightly above the rim of the bowl.

(9) : Cut the last hyacinth (9) to 6 inches and place it between (5) and (6).

Lily of the Valley

(10) : Place the 4 sprigs of lily of the valley (10) as shown in the illustration and diagram.

Greens

(11) : Fill in the spaces between the flowers with leaves (11) cut off the tulips. Use extra greenery to hide the container, if necessary, laying foliage flat at the base of the arrangement.

Variations on a Theme

Once you have learned to make the master arrangement, you can vary it for different occasions and other seasons of the year. The general size and shape will remain the same, but the colors will differ. The directions for assembling are the same too, but you will substitute other flowers, number for number and size for size, according to each new list of materials.

For instance, (4) in the original was a bud 9 inches tall, so (4) in the All-White variation soon to be described will be a bud 9 inches tall —in this case a white rosebud. If you are called upon to substitute a flower which can't rightly be described as full-blown or partly open, simply choose smaller or larger blooms to maintain the relative sizes. The placement of each flower will be the same as in the master arrangement.

All-White, All-Season Arrangement

For many formal occasions this arrangement is an excellent choice, and the flowers are available from your florist at any season. A nice thing about all-white is that it will look beautiful no matter what your color scheme or table appointments. For a very special occasion such as a wedding, you may want to substitute tiny white spray orchids for the sweet peas.

(1) through (6) : white roses

(7) through (9) : white carnations

(10) : 4 sprays of white sweet peas

All-Pink Arrangement

This is exactly the same as the All-White Arrangement except for the colors. Use pink roses, pink carnations and pink sweet peas. For a "Sweet Sixteen" party, use babies'-breath for a filler.

Pink and Blue Arrangement

A baby shower is only one occasion on which to use this dainty color scheme. Try it for a birthday party or luncheon as well.

(1) through (6) : pink roses

(7) through (9) : pink hyacinths or pink geraniums, phlox or peonies

(10) and (11) : about 8 sprays of forget-me-nots

*All-white variation
in square container*

Late Spring Arrangement

Perennial shrubs and flowers are a wonderful inspiration and source of springtime arrangements. Experiment with everything that grows in your garden!

(1) through (6) : purple iris

(7) through (9) : lilac blossoms

(10) : 4 sprays of pink or coral azaleas

(11) : iris leaves

Yellow and Orange Arrangement

This warm and sunny scheme will brighten your table, no matter what the weather.

(1) through (6) : orange zinnias

(7) through (9) : yellow snapdragons

(10) : 4 sprays of tiny yellow chrysanthemums

Midsummer Wild Flower Arrangement

This arrangement and the next one will give you an idea of what you can do with wild flowers. There are so many varieties to choose from, you will find a multitude of lovely combinations, and you can mix them beautifully with garden flowers.

(1) through (6) : Queen Anne's lace

(7) through (9) : wild lupins

(10) : 4 sprays of pink clover

(11) : asparagus fern or wild carrot leaves

Late Summer Wild Flower Arrangement

(1) through (6) : black-eyed Susans

(7) through (9) : goldenrod

(10) : buttercups—use enough to fill in all spaces—or substitute tiny marigolds.

Late Summer Garden Arrangement

(1) through (6) : white phlox

(7) through (9) : lavender phlox (or yellow marigolds if you prefer contrast)

(10) : 4 sprigs of ageratum

Harvest Arrangement

The warm, rusty hues of autumn are lovely against the polished wood of a bare table top.

(1) through (6) : rust-colored pompons

(7) through (9) : oak leaves

(10) : 4 sprays of bittersweet

Christmas arrangement in cake tin

Christmas Arrangement

If you use a cake tin as a container for this arrangement, hide it with a layer of small Christmas tree ornaments—all red or all green would be nice—or with festoons of tinsel.

(1) through (6) : red carnations

(7) through (9) : holly

(10) : 4 sprigs of mistletoe

(11) : small-needled pine twigs

33

Illustration 2

34

ARRANGEMENT IN A TALL VASE FOR FLOOR

It's a little odd that we so seldom think of setting a vase of tall flowers or branches on the floor, but the arrangement works wonders for the decor of any room. Try it in a foyer or entrance hall, or dramatically placed near a stairway.

A tall arrangement such as the one shown in Ill. 2 requires fairly long branches. If branches (1) and (2) are not long enough (they should be three times the height of your vase), attach an extender branch with florist's wire, string or even stout rubber bands. (See the drawing below on the left.) To hold each branch firmly in place in the vase, attach a crosspiece to the branch, as shown on the right, and wedge into place.

The branches you pick—or buy—will not look like those in the illustration, but you can soon remedy that. Cut or trim away the side branches with clippers to get a tall, slim effect. For the more intricate shapes, you

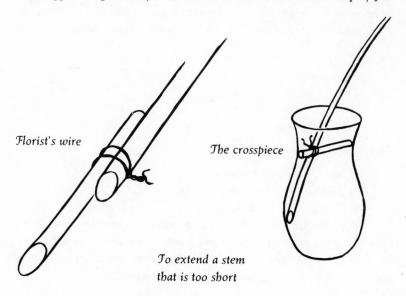

Florist's wire

The crosspiece

To extend a stem that is too short

will probably have to bend some of the branches. Sometimes, it is true, you may be able to get just the right shape by a judicious trimming away of extraneous branches. You can bend any branch quite easily by first soaking it in water to soften it a bit. (See page 23.)

Materials

A Spring Arrangement, Predominantly Yellow

The first robin may not chirp on your window sill, but you'll know spring has really arrived when you bring in pussy willow and forsythia. These are the materials you will need for the arrangement in Ill. 2.

(1) : pussy willow $3\frac{1}{2}$ times the height of your vase, inserted upright.

(2) : pussy willow a little shorter than (1). Place the branch slightly to rear of (1).

(3) : forsythia $\frac{2}{3}$ the height of (1). Insert to left and front of (1).

(4) : forsythia a little shorter than (3), sweeping to the right.

(5) : forsythia the same height as (4), leaning gracefully to front.

(6) through (8) : daffodils of slightly different lengths, the longest being twice the height of the container. Place at base of (1), filling the space between (1) and (4). Fill in with leaves from the daffodils.

Variations

Pink Spring Arrangement

(1) and (2) : English boxwood

(3) through (5) : cherry or plum blossoms

(6) through (8) : pink Amaryllis

To get the same airy effect from the boxwood branches that you get from forsythia, strip off some of the leaves judiciously. This will accentuate the graceful lines as well as the directions of the branches. Bend them to shape according to the directions on page 23.

White Spring Arrangement

This arrangement is quite sophisticated. It would lend grace to an austere color scheme such as red, black and white.

(1) and (2) : pussy willow
(3) through (5) : dogwood
(6) through (8) : Easter lilies

Azalea Arrangement

Some arrangements made with several kinds of flowers in the master plan are equally effective in versions containing only one type. You can use all of one kind of flower for all eight elements of this lovely basic arrangement, or combine different types. If you have a variety of different azaleas, you can combine harmonizing or contrasting colors, but follow the sizes and shapes given in Ill. 2.

Lilac Arrangement

Here we limit our flowers to lilacs, effectively set off with bamboo fronds.

(1) through (3) : bamboo fronds
(4) through (8) : lilacs

Red and White Arrangement

A really eye-catching arrangement, this one will create a splash of color to illuminate a drab corner or dim entrance hall.

(1) and (2) : red gladioli
(3) through (5) : laurel branches
(6) through (8) : white gladioli

Illustration 3

A ladies' luncheon arrangement on an oval table

ARRANGEMENT-WITHOUT-TEARS FOR THE DINING TABLE

This arrangement is so beautiful, so dressy, so impressive—and at the same time so extremely simple and quick—you will almost feel like a charlatan when your friends "Ooh" and "Ah" over it! And when you murmur modestly, "Why it was really nothing at all," you'll be telling the plain, unvarnished truth.

Don't expect your friends not to copy the design shown in Ill. 3, for it explains itself at a glance. One look tells all, as you probably realized when you yourself looked at the illustration. What we actually used in the pictured arrangement are seven crescent-shaped salad dishes arranged in an oval for an oval table, but you should set out your containers to harmonize with the shape of your own table—a square, circle or rectangle, as the case may be.

If you don't happen to have a set of crescent-shaped salad dishes— and they're not exactly standard equipment in most homes—there are many possible substitutes. You can use small vegetable dishes, low sherbet cups, rimmed coasters that will hold water, uniform glass ash trays or whatever you have handy. If the containers are quite small, you may need

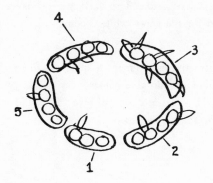

top view

more than seven, but you can best determine this by trying them on your table in advance of making the arrangement.

Pictured in Ill. 3 are red and white azaleas. The white blossoms outnumber the red two to one, so that the dark color provides the accent. The stalks should be cut, their ends clipped (as shown on page 21), and arranged several hours before the guests arrive so the flowers will have time to perk up.

It is hard to say just how many sprigs you will need, as this will depend so much on factors personal to you: the size of your table, how big a centerpiece you want, the size of the individual containers you select, and even the size of the blossoms on the particular variety of azalea you are using. If you are trimming the blossoms from your own bushes, you can pick as many individual sprigs as you think you'll need and simply cut more if necessary. Otherwise, figure on 5 or 6 sprigs of blossoms per saladier, or 3 each for smaller containers. You will also need a very small pin holder for each container unless you happen to be using deep enough dishes to hold the sprigs without danger of their becoming disarranged.

Variations

Gardenias will give a rich, formal look to your table if you want to splurge for a special occasion. The dark, glossy leaves provide all the contrast you need for the waxy white blooms.

Pansies are an attractive addition to a table set for a children's party. Be sure to point out the adorable pansy faces to the young guests. And here's a thought: Use plastic cups and give each child a pansy arrangement to take home for a souvenir.

Red, White and Blue Arrangement For a gay and patriotic Fourth of July, use red and white geraniums combined with blue delphiniums. Use red and white roses (or carnations) with blue violets for an "election night" party.

Informal Wild Flower Arrangements will add charm to your table all through the warm months. Just pick whatever is growing—daisies, clover, Indian paintbrush—in profusion, and arrange in the magic square or circle which best suits your dining table.

Flowering Shrubs lend themselves to the arrangement shown in Ill. 3. Lilacs would be beautiful with their heart-shaped green leaves for accent. Try, too, hydrangeas, snowballs, Deutzia, or rambler roses.

Illustration 4

"TRÈS CHIC" ARRANGEMENT

The handsome, rather stylized arrangement pictured in Ill. 4 has an extremely professional look to it. Place it on something low, like this slatted bench, or on a shelf of a room divider.

You need some sort of a large, shallow container for this arrangement. The one shown in Ill. 4 is terra cotta, unglazed outside with an aqua glaze inside, about 8 inches by 12 inches in size.

Included in this arrangement are 8 or 10 shiny Japanese pebbles. They add so much flavor, you will surely want to use them again and again with this and many other arrangements. You will probably feel the same about the driftwood (or seaweed) tree which forms the group's tall main ingredient. You can buy such a tree already anchored to a receptacle, or if you have access to a lake, river or seashore, you may be able to find one yourself.

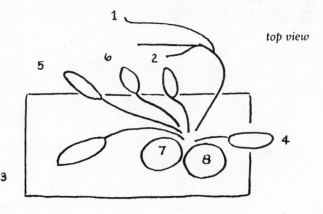

top view

Materials

(1) : seaweed or driftwood tree anchored firmly in place to the right of center

(2) through (6) : sprays of "Christmas Cheer," a long-stemmed succulent of brilliant red

(7) and (8) : full-blown grey-green hen and chicken plants set off by shiny grey and black Japanese pebbles

Variations

Begonia Variation

(2) through (6) : begonia stems with small white blossoms

(7) and (8) : pink camellias with shiny dark leaves behind them, arranged with white pebbles

Dry Arrangement

(1) : beige driftwood if possible

(2) through (6) : clusters and vine (red and beige) of wood cherry

(7) and (8) : 3 large straw flowers (1 red, 1 orange, 1 yellow) used with beige pebbles

JOYOUS HARVEST ARRANGEMENT

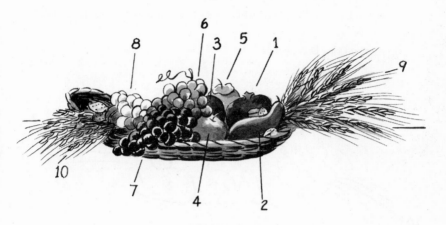

Illustration 5

There is a certain pleasure about handling the ripe fruits of the earth which even the veriest city-dweller is bound to feel—a primitive pleasure linking us in time with our earliest ancestors. The pleasure of a bountiful harvest after a year of labor is always joyous.

Fruit always makes a pleasing centerpiece for the dinner table, especially at Thanksgiving and Christmas time. The long oval basket of straw used in Ill. 5 carries out the harvest theme, but you can use a silver bread tray if elegance is your keynote.

Materials

(1) : dark red pomegranate
(2) : brown Anjou pear

(3) and (4) : red and green apples

(5) : orange persimmon

(6) : red Tokay grapes—a large bunch

(7) : dark purple Concord grapes—a medium-sized bunch

(8) : light green grapes—a small bunch

(9) and (10) : sheaves of wheat. (9) is equal in length to the basket, and (10) is ⅔ as long.

Nuts and raw cranberries

side view

The fruit goes into place first; if you wish, you can place it on a bed of finely shredded dark green tissue paper. Place the pomegranate high in the right end of the basket and tuck the Anjou pear under it. The apples go in next. Balance a bright orange persimmon on top of the apples (use an extra apple if necessary), and mass a large bunch of Malaga or Tokay grapes partly over the apples, so that they cascade down into the bottom of the receptacle.

If the light green grapes and the dark purple Concords do not fill the basket completely, you may have to place 1 or 2 small apples, oranges or tangerines in the bottom of the left end of the basket beneath the grapes. The purple grapes droop over the front of the basket, and the green grapes extend a bit beyond the left rear rim.

46

Finally, insert the tied sheaves of wheat. Lift the pear gently just enough to insert (9) under it, so the wheat sheaf will curve upward. Insert (10) under the green grapes, (8), bending it forward and down over the rim of the basket.

Fill in the spaces, indicated in the diagram accompanying Ill. 5 by the dark spots, with walnuts and almonds in the shell, and raw cranberries if you have them.

Illustration 6

48

"CHI-CHI" ARRANGEMENT

We call the arrangement pictured in Ill. 6 "chi-chi" because the term is so often used by decorators to describe something stunning and unusual.

Our Ill. 6 shows a boat-shaped ceramic container, although any long, oval-shaped dish—a cut glass or crystal celery boat or a bread tray of silver—would do as well. (Remember this one if ever you need a "bon voyage" arrangement!)

The free-form mat and the glass balls add charm to the arrangement and increase the sea-going illusion. Cut the mat out of felt, burlap or an interestingly textured inexpensive straw place mat. As for the crystal balls, you buy them at the florist's shop or at a dime store, and they're a worth-while investment. They add a sure-fingered touch to this and many other arrangements.

Materials

Hosta Leaves

(1): The longest leaf should be 1½ times the length of the container. Shape it gently under water to achieve a sweeping, oarlike shape. Anchor it to the pin holder and bring it forward and right, over the edge of the container.

(2): Use the widest leaf for this saillike effect. It is approximately ⅔ the length of (1), or perhaps a little longer. Set it firmly upright.

(3): Cut to ⅔ the length of (2). Set it so that its point tapers slightly in the opposite direction from (2).

Snapdragons, White

Here is the contrast which is the essence of this arrangement—the soft full white blossoms against the stark hosta leaves.

(4): slightly shorter than (3), upright and to the rear.

(5) and (6) are shorter than (4) and bend slightly away from (4) toward the front.

(7) : shorter still than (4), this flower bends low over the rim of the bowl, following the general direction of (1).

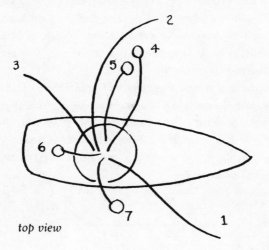

top view

Variations

Red Arrangement

This deep red version would be tremendously effective against a white wall, daringly handsome against a pink wall!

(1) through (3) : canna lily leaves

(4) through (7) : dark red sprays of heather

Miniature Arrangements

Use a small oval ash tray, or pin tray or any dainty little container no longer than 3 inches. Take a small lump of florist's clay and anchor it off-center. Then, using a toothpick or matchstick, poke small holes in the clay in which to insert the flowers, so that water will reach the stems.

Miniature Red Arrangement

    (1) through (3) : Montbretia leaves

    (4) through (7) : flowers of Montbretia

Miniature White Arrangement

For a bridal shower, baby shower or wedding breakfast, individual flower arrangements which also serve as place-card holders are most charming. These tiny arrangements leave the center of the table free, so that you can place the gifts there in an upside-down umbrella, or perhaps, for a baby shower, in a plastic bathtub or a clothes hamper for baby's things. In the case of a wedding breakfast, the cake can hold the place of honor.

    (1) through (3) : leaves of lily of the valley

    (4) through (7) : sprays of lily of the valley

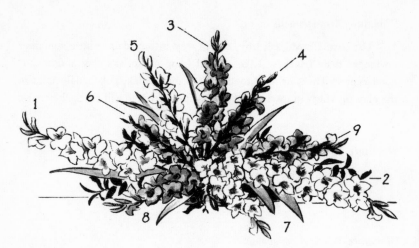

Illustration 7

CLASSIC GLADIOLUS ARRANGEMENT FOR A
FORMAL DINNER

This long, low floral arrangement (Ill. 7) with its simple beauty is always in good taste in any sort of decor. Its beauty lies in the understatement of the flowers themselves, rather than the originality of a striking container or a daring departure in shape.

Although this arrangement is 20 inches long, and can be extended if necessary to 30 or 36 inches, the container itself need be no longer than 8 or 10 inches. Gladioli form the basis for this design, and their strong, stiff stems extend well beyond the container. If you remember to add water frequently, this arrangement will last for days.

To begin with, shape chicken wire in a dome over your container and wedge it in place with florist's clay. Or else use the green plastic foam blocks as holders. If you want to "make assurance double sure," use both wire and holders.

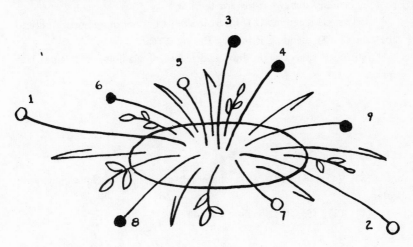

Pink- and Rose-Colored Arrangement

(3), (4), (6), (8), (9) : deep rose-colored gladioli

(1), (2), (5), (7) : pink gladioli

You will have to insert the flowers in consecutive order because their size and weight make it necessary to balance them as you go along. That is the reason that the colors are not consecutively grouped by number:

(1) : about 12 inches long; insert it almost horizontally to the rear and left.

(2) : about 12 inches long; insert it almost horizontally to the front, right.

(3) : about 10 inches tall. Insert it upright in the center.

(4) : 8 inches tall. Insert it to right of (3), bending it to the rear.

(5) : 6 inches tall. Insert it to the left of (3), bending to the front.

(6) : 5 inches tall. Insert it next to (5), bending it rather sharply to the rear.

(7) : same length as (6). Insert it next to (4), bending it toward the front.

(8) : 8 inches long. Insert it almost but not quite horizontally in front of (1), bending somewhat toward the left.

(9) : same length as (8). Insert it almost but not quite horizontally to the rear of (2), bending it toward the right rear.

Fill in all spaces with shortened leaves of gladiolus and laurel leaf sprigs.

Variations

Chartreuse and Yellow

(3), (4), (6), (8), (9) : shamrock gladioli, a luscious chartreuse color

(1), (2), (5), (7) : yellow gladioli

Orange and Brownish-Red

(3), (4), (6), (8), (9) : orange gladioli

(1), (2), (5), (7) : brownish-red gladioli

Substitute red dwarf maple leaves for the laurel leaves.

Lavender and White

(3), (4), (6), (8), (9) : lavender gladioli

(1), (2), (5), (7) : white gladioli

Multi-colored Arrangement

(3), (4), (6), (8), (9) : coral-pink gladioli

(1), (2), (5), (7) : white gladioli

Use sprays of small yellow pompons as fillers.

If your table is very long and you want a longer arrangement than the one in Ill. 7, you will need only 4 more stalks and some extra filler.

54

Increase the size of (1) and (2) to 15 or 20 inches, depending on just how long an arrangement you need. All the other sizes will remain the same. The 4 extra stalks should be about midway in length between the new size of (1) and (2) and the size of (8) and (9).

For filler you will have to use flowers as well as laurel leaves. Pompons, carnations, African daisies, and sweet peas will all be suitable. Keep them low in the middle, and let them extend to the right and left to fill in the ends of the design as much as possible.

PERMANENT ARRANGEMENT FOR
A CORNER TABLE OR SHELF

No water is necessary for the arrangement pictured in Ill. 8, and "no fair" moving it around. It belongs in a corner, with only one face toward the public, and there it will stay happily, needing no further attention. (Dust it occasionally by using the light blower from the wrong end of your vacuum cleaner, or just by blowing on it yourself.) The master arrangement is a silvery blue-green which will be effective with almost any color scheme, but is particularly handsome in a room that is predominantly blue. There is a variation in warmer tones, and a summery green one as well.

The shallow container can be oblong or possibly oval or a free-form —any shape that is longer than it is wide. The bamboo mat on which the arrangement rests, while not vital, is effective. Attach a heavy pin holder to the right rear of the container with florist's clay.

Materials

Globe Thistle

(Steel-blue balls and light grey-green stalks and leaves)

(1): about 1½ times the length of the container. Insert it upright in the center of a pin holder.

(2) has a smaller globe but is slightly taller than (1). Insert it behind and to the right of (1).

(3): slightly shorter than (1). Insert it to the right of (2), leaning somewhat forward.

(4): shorter than (3). Insert it to the left of (1), bending toward the left.

Pineapple Top

(5): Slice the top off a fresh pineapple and place it at the base of the arrangement facing front and right.

Illustration 8

Yucca Leaves

(Silvery pale green)

(6): slightly taller than (2). Insert it between (2) and (3).

(7): a long yucca leaf, approximately 2 times longer than the dish. Insert it between (1) and (4), swaying toward the left.

(8): ½ the length of (7). Insert it low in front, bending forward over the rim of the dish in a graceful curve.

Rocks

Two dark bluish rocks, or grey with a blue cast, complete the arrangement. Place the large rock at the base near the pin holder, and the smaller one to the left, fairly far from other elements in the arrangement.

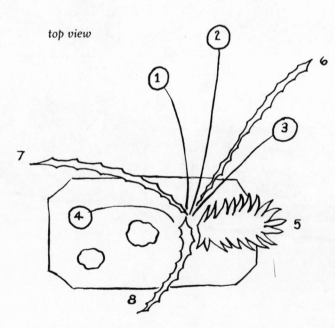

top view

Variations

Warm Beige Tones

(1) through (4) : either dried straw flowers in golden brown shades or dried goldenrod

(5) : ground cherry pods

(6) through (8) : dried Dracaena leaves

1 large and 1 small sandy-colored rock

Green Summer Arrangement

As its name implies, this variation is not permanent. However, having learned to make the master arrangement, you will want to use your skill to put together this summertime display.

(1) through (4) : green thistles before they flower

(5) : hen and chicken plant

(6) through (8) : bells of Ireland

1 large and 1 small greenish-grey rock or 2 moss-covered rocks

Illustration 9

Ice bucket arrangement—to flank a painting or mirror

SOPHISTICATED MANTELPIECE ARRANGEMENT

Because of its shape, the arrangement pictured in Ill. 9 belongs on the left side of the mantel, flanking a painting or mirror. If you intend to keep a rather tall arrangement on your mantel at all times, you might consider hanging a mirror or painting off-center to the right. If you have an ice bucket of teak, it makes a handsome container, but of course not everyone has such a bucket. And of those who do, perhaps not everyone can spare it for a flower arrangement. In fact, not everyone has a mantelpiece.

Still, the arrangement is too handsome to dismiss altogether. Fortunately, like all the others in this book, it is adaptable. For example, you can use a tall basket with a handle in place of the ice bucket. Set a tin can or a glass tumbler or jar inside to hold water. You can even use a vase without a handle. Furthermore, you can set the arrangement on a buffet, sideboard, chest of drawers, secretary or even on top of the television if you must.

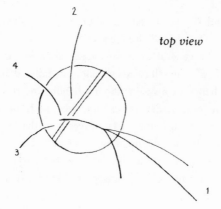

top view

Materials

(1) : full spray of Scotch heather (*Calluna vulgaris*) 2½ times the height of the receptacle. Wedge a stout piece of branch tightly across the left inside rim of receptacle and secure (1) to this crosspiece with florist's wire or adhesive tape. Here is how it is done:

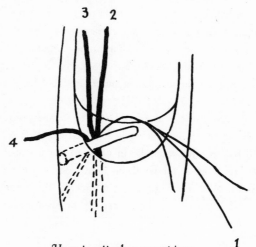

How to attach a crosspiece

(2), (3) and (4) are magnolia branches whose sizes and shapes are described below. Discard all dead leaves and clip any branches that do not conform to the general direction of the main branch.

(2) : branch of magnolia leaves somewhat taller than the handle, or about twice the height of a vase without a handle. Insert it to the rear and arrange it so that some of the leaves hang over the front of the handle.

(3) : a shorter branch than (2). Insert it to the left front, bending sharply over rim. If you do not have a sharply bent branch, shape it gently under water until you achieve the desired curve.

(4) is a smaller branch still. Insert it behind (3) so that it follows the general line of (2).

This arrangement of dark magnolia leaves and purple heather with the rich brown-orange of the teak bucket is particularly effective against a dull white background.

Variations

Light Arrangement Against a Dark Wall

    (1) : spray of white clematis
    (2) through (4) : large bamboo leaves

Ritzy 'Rangement

    (1) : brown and yellow spray orchids
    (2) through (4) : large caladium leaves

Autumn

    (1) : spray of dark red and orange pyracantha berries.

    (2) through (4) : select branches of oak leaves that are predominantly yellow and red with a touch of green still remaining. Trim off the lower leaves, leaving clumps on the end.

Other Ideas

    Laurel or bay leaves with a spray of wisteria
    Chestnut leaves with a spray of forsythia
    Walnut leaves with a spray of dogwood
    And for Christmas, holly leaves with poinsettias

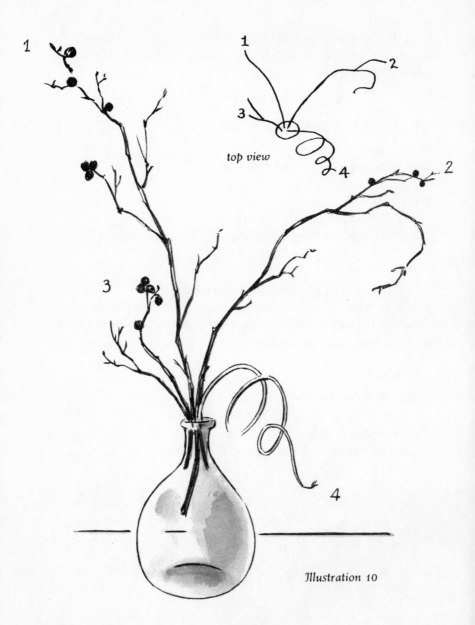

top view

Illustration 10

SIMPLE, PERMANENT DRY ARRANGEMENT

This arrangement (Ill. 10) consists of so few materials, it is no wonder that the container is an especially important part of it. Used in Ill. 10 is a sea-green flask. To be sure, you do not need a bottle of exactly this size, shape and color, but then, neither can you use an empty soft drink bottle. If you do not have some sort of narrow-mouthed bottle of interesting color, shape, and perhaps texture to display on a buffet or console, save this arrangement until you do. And keep it in mind if you get near an antique shop!

Materials

Bittersweet

(1): a branch of bittersweet 3 times the height of the bottle, rather straight.

(2): a twisted branch of bittersweet about the same size as (1) but trimmed or bent to fold interestingly back on itself.

(3): a short stalk of bittersweet, perhaps one you have trimmed off (1) or (2).

Bryonia or Grape Vine

(4): a spiral of bryonia vine, about 3 or 4 times the height of the bottle. First soak the vine, and then twine it around a slender olive jar. Tie or tape it to the jar and allow it to dry out completely. Remove it carefully from the bottle and gently pat it into shape, trimming it if it is too long.

Wedge the 4 elements firmly into place, using a small cork cut to size for a plug if necessary. Or else cut a few 1-inch lengths of bittersweet stem and wedge them into the neck of the bottle.

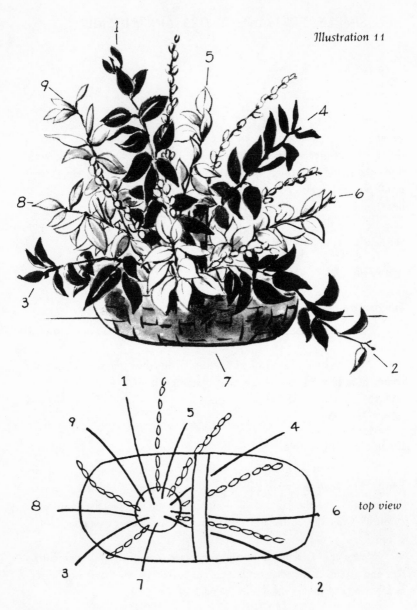

Illustration 11

top view

66

A BOUNTEOUS BASKET OF LEAVES

Sunday is a good time to prepare the arrangement shown in Ill. 11, for we designed it especially to grace your breakfast-nook window, or kitchen counter. Put it in place on Sunday night to dispel those Monday morning blues!

You can use a pin holder for this arrangement if it is large and heavy enough to hold branches. If you do not have a large, heavy pin holder, you can combine two or three smaller ones, as illustrated here. Place the holder, or group of holders, in a low bowl, to the left of the basket handle.

For purposes of clarity, the main branches (1) through (4) are drawn in black. Actually, all the branches are hemlock. Cut them at an angle, as shown on page 21.

Materials

Hemlock Branches

(1): about 1½ times the length of basket. Insert it in the center, upright but bending slightly to the left.

(2): same size as (1). Insert it to the right, bending gracefully forward so that the leaves almost trail onto the table.

(3): about ⅔ the size of (1). Insert it at the left, low over the rim of the basket.

(4): same size as (3) but with a secondary branch attached. Insert it at the right rear, bending toward the back.

(5): ½ the size of (1). Insert it at the center, bending toward the rear along the handle of the basket.

(6): same length as 5. Insert it between (2) and (4).

(7): slightly shorter than (6). Place it in front, bending upward along the handle.

(8) and (9): same size as (3). Use these two branches to fill in

the space between (1) and (3), following the general directions of (1) and (3).

Pussy Willow

Arrange 8 twigs of pussy willow in pairs and use them as fillers. They should be a little taller than (1) but necessarily uniform in size. Insert one each between (4) and (5); (2) and (7); (8) and (9); (9) and (1); (1) and (5); 2 branches between (4) and (6); 1 behind (7).

Variations

Spruce for the branches and cattails for filler.

Autumn leaves in brilliant colors, and ilex to add a green touch, but not as a filler.

Magnolia branches with bittersweet for filler.

Any attractive leafy branch with evergreen for a filler.

1 large 5" holder or a combination holder

MIDWINTER "PICK-ME-UP"

Illustration 12

Particularly good for the barren winter months when your garden is quite bare, the arrangement shown in Ill. 12 will serve two purposes. Not only will it cheer up a simple family dinner, but it will also prevent you from serving a fattening gravy, for your receptacle is the gravy boat!

You can use philodendron for your greens, and this arrangement gives you a good way to use the parts you trim away when you give your house plants a "hair-cut." In fact, it will start the shoots on the path to rerooting. Or, you may want to bring in greens from bushes or trees, or buy some at the florist's shop to give the arrangement more of a lift by adding a new note to your decor.

The leaves are all of one variety, but (1) and (3) are shown in black for the sake of clarity. Use a pin holder in the gravy boat.

Materials

(1): about ⅓ the length of the gravy boat. Insert it to the left, bending toward the left front.

(2): Use a double branch or your fullest branch. It should be slightly longer than (1). Insert it to the rear, bending toward the right.

(3) is your dramatic accent, about 1 and ⅔ the length of the container. Insert it in the front and let it arch to the right front, bending low over the rim of the gravy boat.

Variations

Try laurel branches, rhododendrons, English ivy, Virginia creeper, holly leaves, or any other greens that strike your fancy.

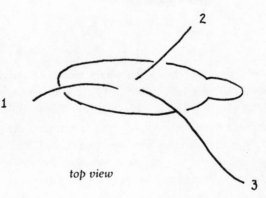

top view

COFFEE TABLE CHARMER

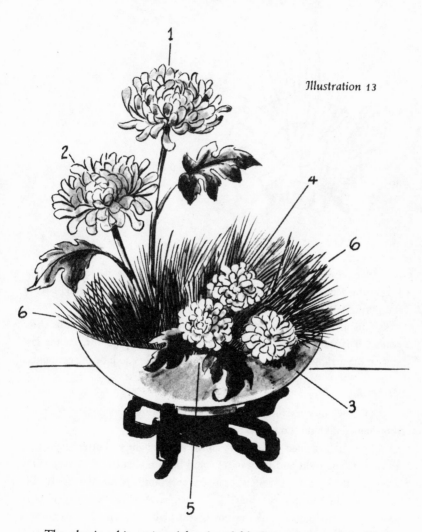

Illustration 13

The classic white oriental bowl and black wooden stand in Ill. 13 are easy to find and inexpensive to buy if you don't already own an

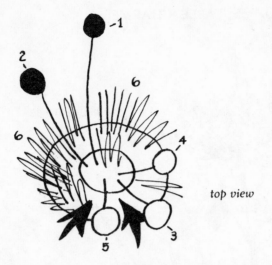

top view

attractive bowl of suitable size and shape. A simple ceramic bowl or perhaps a deep vegetable serving dish from your dinnerware might serve the purpose.

This arrangement is also quite satisfactory in a makeshift, unsightly container if you are going to place it on something quite low. As the last step in the arrangement, simply add enough greenery to hide the container.

Materials

(1) : white chrysanthemum, full-blown, whose height is 1½ times the diameter of the bowl. Place it to left center.

(2) : half-opened white chrysanthemum, slightly shorter than (1). Place it to the right and back of (1) and bend it slightly away from (1).

(3) through (5) : yellow pompon chrysanthemums of slightly differing heights, the tallest being ½ the height of (1). Place (3) leaning over the front right rim of the bowl, and place (4) and (5) to form a triangle as per the diagram accompanying Ill. 13.

(6) : branches of long-needled pine to fill in according to the diagram.

72

Variations

Pink and Green Arrangement

This is always a happy color scheme. Actually, you can use dahlias or mums as well as asters. And how about carnations?

(1) and (2) : light pink asters
(3) through (5) : deep pink asters
(6) : English ivy

Springtime Yellow Arrangement

Old friends in a new setting!
(1) and (2) : yellow tulips
(3) through (5) : jonquils
(6) : sprigs of forsythia

Miniature Arrangement for Early Spring

(1) and (2) : crocus blossoms, full-blown, in white or yellow
(3) through (5) : Use either crocus buds or snow drops.
(6) : Use violets for filler, making 4 little bunches held by rubber bands, or use young dandelion leaves for filler.

Sweetheart Miniature Arrangement

This little gem of an arrangement would be charming on a breakfast tray for a special occasion or for a convalescent.

(1) and (2) : full-blown sweetheart roses
(3) through (5) : sweetheart rosebuds, with their leaves used for filler

Christmas Arrangement

You can decorate this variation with small balls from the Christmas tree or bits of shiny silver tinsel.

(1) and (2) : poinsettias
(3) through (5) : matching red carnations
(6) : holly or pine branches for filler

Illustration 14

CASUAL, BUT NOT CARELESS

Perhaps you have only gone to a florist for the kind of "duty" floral offerings for which price, and what is seemly, play the most important part in your decision of what to buy. If so, you have a surprise in store for you. As a flower arranger, you will be buying not by the dozen, but by the piece, and you needn't hesitate or be embarrassed to ask for 2 of this and 3 of that. Furthermore, you needn't pay long-stemmed prices for flowers which are going to be cut down to size anyway, nor for geometrically straight stems when a curve or two doesn't matter. Gladioli, for example, are sometimes what the florist terms "cripples"—blooms on crooked stalks—which may be admirable for your purposes and which should cost less than the upright specimens.

Don't hesitate to ask any florist for exactly the kind of blooms you want for an arrangement—buds, bloom and bud on one stalk, and so on. Far from looking down his nose at you, he will be more than happy to serve you according to your desires, and he may even offer helpful suggestions or give you professional hints.

The arrangement of roses in a medium-wide-mouthed vase shown in Ill. 14 looks quite simple. It *is* quite simple. But there's more to it than meets the eye, if "less" can, indeed, be "more." What we mean is this: Careful arrangement makes 5 roses look the part of a dozen! For a writing desk, an end table, the dresser in your guest room, or any spot that needs the cheery effect of roses from your garden (or from the florist during fall or winter), this simple, gracious arrangement will fill the bill.

The container for this arrangement should be about 6 inches high. A small glass pitcher or a tall creamer might take the place of the vase. If the neck is too wide, crisscross it with strips of sticky cellophane tape. This will keep the flowers just where you want them.

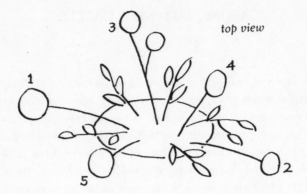

top view

Materials

Red, Pink, Yellow or White Roses with Excess Leaves Trimmed Away

(1): Choose a large full-bown rose and cut it to twice the height of the container. (See page 27 for instructions on how to open up a flower under water.) Place the flower to the left rear.

(2): a partly opened rose cut to ⅔ the height of (1). Place it to the right and rear of (1).

(3): This is a half-opened rose with a bud attached, slightly shorter than (1) and placed directly to the rear of it.

(4): slightly taller than (2). Insert it in the center, gently bending it toward the front over the rim of the container.

(5): This is the shortest of all, just a little taller than the vase. Place it in front, to the left of (4).

Trim away all the leaves except two sprigs per stem, as shown in the diagram which accompanies Ill. 14. The leaves will fill the open areas in the arrangement.

Variations

Dahlias, chrysanthemums, asters, hydrangeas—any flower with a full round bloom lends itself delightfully to this treatment.

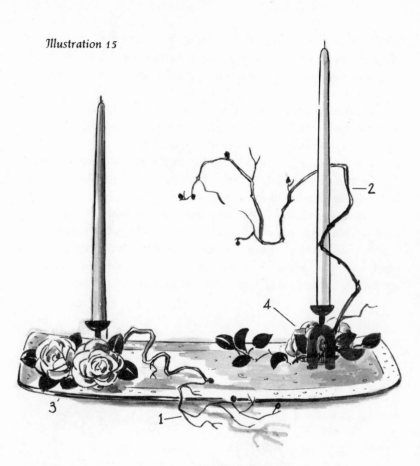

Illustration 15

CANDLE CENTERPIECE FOR A LONG TABLE

You can use the arrangement pictured in Ill. 15 as a centerpiece at lunch or dinner, but its best use is probably to decorate the table between meals—a far more difficult assignment. It would be equally at home on a

77

low buffet or a low modern mantelpiece. This is another arrangement which requires more in the way of accessories than floral materials. However, once you own a vase similar in size and shape to the green-colored bubble glass tray shown in Ill. 15, and suitable candlestick holders, you need spend only a few cents on flowers to keep the arrangement always fresh and handsome. The first two elements are permanent (bittersweet), so you only have to renew the 4 flowers at the base.

The candlesticks in Ill. 15 are alike in design but different in size. You can achieve practically the same effect by using identical candlesticks with matching candles of different heights.

Notice that the tray illustrated here does not hold water. Use two small self-contained pin holders and be sure to add water frequently. If you do not own this type of container, you can use the empty tins in which anchovies, deviled ham and other foods are packaged with small pin holders anchored into them with florist's clay.

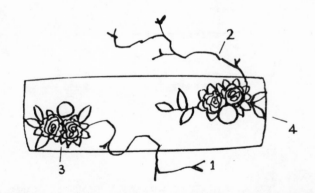

top view

Materials

(1) and (2): bittersweet. Select interestingly curved branches or trim and coax them into shape. Insert (1) in front of the candletsick on the left, and use cellophane tape to attach the bittersweet to the right candle to hold it up. Insert (2) at the left and let it sweep forward.

(3) and (4) are pairs of deep red camellias. Place one set in front of the left candlestick and the other pair on the opposite side of the right candle, so that the arrangement will look pretty from both sides.

Variations

In place of the camellias, you can use gardenias, tiger lilies, Talisman roses, dahlias, chrysanthemums, poppies, water lilies, or similar-sized flowers. In the spring you can replace the bittersweet with flowering fruit branches such as cherry, plum or apple.

For an extra-special occasion, brown and white orchids would be very impressive. If you wish to present a corsage to a guest of honor in a charming and novel way, let the corsage live a double life. First use it as part of the arrangement, with a few pretty pebbles underneath, so that the arrangement will still look nice after you make the presentation.

SPECTACULAR OLD-FASHIONED BOUQUET

"Luscious" is the word for the arrangement shown in Ill. 16, just luscious! What else can we say? The lines are lovely, the colors are wonderful, but the accent is on the beauty of the blossoms themselves.

The container pictured here is a white cookie jar, but if you don't have one, a 46-ounce fruit-juice can will do the trick. Just slip a cylinder of white poster paper over it. Simplicity is necessary to accent the brilliance of the flowers.

To hold the flowers in place, anchor a small frozen-fruit-juice can firmly to the bottom of the inside of the receptacle, using florist's clay. You will later fill the whole jar, vase or can with water, not just the little inner can which holds the flower stems. Start by standing the first 4 or 5 elements in the central container, so that they will brace one another, and then re-arrange them into position according to the directions below.

Materials

Blue Delphiniums

(1): $2\frac{1}{2}$ times the height of the container, upright in the center, bending slightly to the right.

(2): $\frac{2}{3}$ the height of (1), placed to the front and left of (1).

(3): slightly shorter than (2), placed to the right of (2) and bending to the right.

Plum-Colored Asters

(4): $\frac{2}{3}$ the height of (2). Place it between (1) and (3).

(5): slightly shorter than (4), below and slightly to the left of (4).

(6): slightly shorter than (5), below (5), facing to the right.

(7): slightly shorter than (6), bending to the left over the rim of the container to the left of (6).

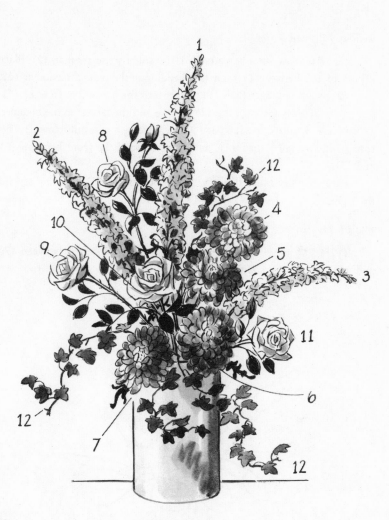

Illustration 16

Yellow Talisman Roses

(8) : This rose has a bud attached. It is slightly shorter than (2). Place it back of (1) between (1) and (2), bending in the same direction as (2).

(9) : slightly longer than (5). Insert it to the left and in front of (2).

(10) : This is the most full-blown rose and the largest in the bouquet. (Again, see the directions on page 27 for making a rose full-blown.) This rose is slightly taller than (5), and bends toward the front between (9) and (5).

(11) : slightly taller than (6). Place it next to (6), bending toward the right.

English Ivy

(12) : 2½ times the height of the container. Insert it between (7) and (9), bending gracefully down to the left.

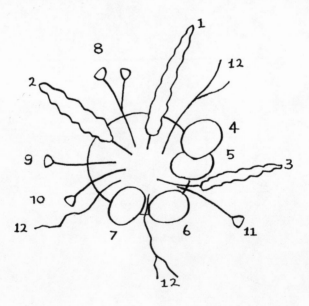

top view

(13): ⅔ the height of (12). Insert it under (6) and (7), bending down and away toward the right.

(14): same size as (12). Insert it between (1) and (4), bending very slightly toward the right rear.

Variations

As you can imagine, the combinations of flowers possible for this kind of arrangement are infinite. Instead of giving you many specific variations, therefore, we will just suggest replacements or alternates for each type of flower. Cut them to the same relative sizes and place them according to the preceding directions.

For the delphiniums, for instance, you can substitute stock, gladioli, snapdragons, lupin, or any long spiky bloom.

In place of the asters—well, where can we begin? Besides all the related flowers like mums and pompons, you can choose any compact flower of about the same size—carnations and roses, of course, African daisies, coriopsis, tulips, even purple flags, though they are hardly compact.

As for the Talisman roses, you can replace them with any large rose, or for that matter, with any of the flowers mentioned in the paragraph just above! We've given you a few suggestions. And here are some additional ones.

Springtime

    (1) through (3): lilacs
    (4) through (7): tulips
    (8) through (11): columbine
    (12) through (14): tulip leaves

Summertime

    (1) through (3): bells of Ireland
    (4) through (7): ruby-red dahlias
    (8) through (11): white Shasta daisies
  (12) through (14): English ivy

Wild Flower Arrangement

    (1) through (3): wild lupin or Indian paintbrush
    (4) through (7): field daisies
    (8) through (11): poppies
  (12) through (14): pond grass

3. Idea Section

Sometimes the best way to put over a general idea is by being specific, and this section contains a great many rather special, very specific little arrangements. Chances are these will act only as springboards. You won't be able to make more than 1 or 2 of them without rushing out to buy special containers plus odds and ends of bric-a-brac, or trays, or doilies or who knows what. But the whole purpose of this section is simply to give you ideas!

We hope, as you read through the following pages, that you will find yourself thinking, again and again, "Why, I can't do *exactly* that arrangement, but it gives me an idea!"

FRUITFUL ARRANGEMENTS

Some people seem to have a knack for the little touch that means so much, and so can you. It's just a matter of doing something "special" a few times and then, instead of a "big deal," it becomes a habit. Take the matter of fruit and flowers. What teen-ager would go for a sickeningly sweet soft drink when he could pick up a fresh polished apple from his desk?

House guests will rave about your ingenuity and your hospitality if you leave an eye-tempting, appetite-tempting arrangement in the guest room for a before-bed snack. But you don't have to wait for special occasions or special guests; once you get in the *habit* of teaming a piece of fruit or two with a flower or two, you'll find yourself doing it often. Leave these fragrant offerings near the master's easy chair, the telephone, the "teevee" settee.

Illustration 17a

In Ill. 17A, a flat, free-form container, glazed turquoise on the inside, offers up a golden delicious apple, a purple plum and an apricot at one end, balanced by a sunflower at the other end. A container with a built-in pin holder is filled with water for the flowers. If you don't have such a container, use a small round can—for example, the type in which tuna is packed—with a 1-inch pin holder inside. (See the drawing below.)

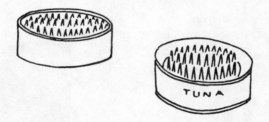

That's the idea. Now, let your mind wander over the possible containers your house provides, the flowers available and the fruit in the "fridge." What will *you* combine with what?

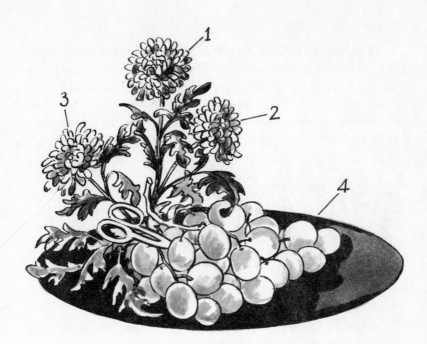

Illustration 17b

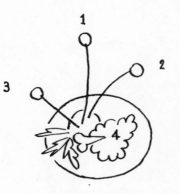

top view

In Ill. 17B, using the same type of holder as above on an oval tray of black lacquer, we show an arrangement of 3 lavender asters, each with a few leaves. Alongside, spilling out in cornucopia fashion, is a luscious bunch of light green grapes. Add a pair of silver grape scissors, or a small pair of sewing scissors, and who will fail to nibble?

Variations

You've probably thought yourself of several possible variations on the fruit theme already. Just to make sure, however, that you think of flowers and arrangements every time you wheel your wagon through the fruit department of the supermarket, or open up your refrigerator, here are a few mouth-watering suggestions:

Substitute yellow flowers (jonquils, roses, mums, zinnias, marigolds, cosmos, goldenrod, primroses, black-eyed Susan, etc.) with any of these fruits—one or two of a kind or in any combination: bananas, apricots, yellow Delicious apples. Or, use purple plums or purple grapes for a contrasting instead of harmonizing arrangement. Or, team up the yellow flowers with tangerines or oranges.

Use red flowers (roses, carnations, salvia, begonias, or red autumn leaves) with red-cheeked Bartlett pears.

Instead of flowers, use all green foliage (ivy, philodendron, any evergreen or leaves from any shrub or tree, or even celery stalks with the leaves on) with a peeled carrot and a brilliant red tomato or perhaps a few crimson radishes.

ETERNAL TRIANGLE

If you have expensive tastes but a limited pocketbook, the arrangement shown in Ill. 18 solves everything. Take a tall goblet, one leaf and 3 posies and voila! You've done it again! In fact, you may well want to do this one twice—for a pair of night tables!

Materials

(1) : a caladium leaf about twice the height of the goblet

(2) through (4) : carnations (the color is up to you) of slightly differing sizes. The tallest (2) is twice the height of the goblet, and quite straight. (3) bends somewhat toward the left and nests within the hollow of the leaf, while (4) droops gracefully to the right.

If you make a second arrangement, for a night table, for example, reverse the directions of the flowers, left-to-right.

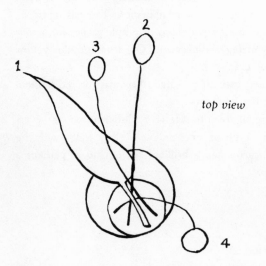

top view

Illustration 18

WHAT-NOT GRAB BAG

Have you ever noticed how easy it is not to really *see* things in a familiar room? When your decor remains static, your eye tends to accept it as a matter of course. How often do you consciously feast your eyes on the beautiful pieces you have so lovingly collected?

"Constantly," you will be able to answer once you get into the habit of sparkling up your lovely things with fresh flowers and greenery. In Ill. 19 we give you four ideas, in hopes that each one will multiply into many others as you incorporate them into your thinking.

Box A

Illustration 19

Box B

Illustration 19

Box A

Take a copper or brass butter warmer and add 1 branch of striped philodendron, English ivy or morning glory vine. A nice and unusual way to hold the greenery in place is to weight it with a smooth pebble collected from the beach or the bottom of a stream.

Box B

Place 4 tiny marigolds in a stemmed glass, or 4 larger marigolds in a water goblet—depending on the size of the piece of bric-a-brac you use to flank the arrangement. Trim off the lower leaves. You can also use daisies, petunias, sweet William, small mums, zinnias, cosmos, asters, anemones—why go on? You can use *anything!*

Box C

Illustration 19

Box C

Take a pitcher and a bread basket (the "thou" is optional). Add 5 tea roses impaled on a pin holder in a small container (remember the tuna can!) so that they just seem to be lying there casually. If you have a silver pitcher, use it! How the silver will gleam!

(For this arrangement, also try primrose, anemone, camellia or tiger lily.)

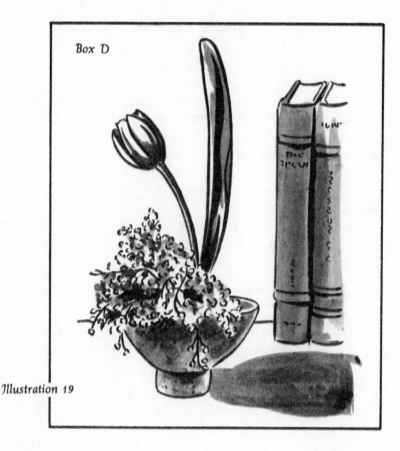

Box D

Illustration 19

Box D

Shown here is a small stoneware container from the Orient, but you might use instead a small ceramic bowl made by your child in kindergarten or any other type of small bowl. Make it alive and vital by adding a few flowers: a tulip, 1 broad tulip leaf and a spray of mimosa, all impaled on a small pin holder.

Attractive variations might be 1 daffodil and leaf with a spray of acacia, or 1 iris and leaf with a spray of heather.

DANISH MODERN

Let a lily be your label! From early spring onward, lilies and iris and narcissus follow one another perennially in rich profusion, but you don't need "a crowd, a host of golden daffodils" or even a dozen blooms. Ill. 20 shows how handsome only two flowers and a bud can appear.

Standing austere and alone, backed by the sabre of a leaf, the Amaryllis illustrated here allows one's mind to dwell on the simple perfection of the star-shaped blossoms.

Be sure to change the water daily, for the crystal-clear liquid in the graceful bottle completes this simple, no-fuss arrangement for a desk or bookcase.

Materials

(1) : partly opened flower and bud, facing left.

(2) : fully opened flower, slightly shorter than (1), facing front.

(3) : leaf, somewhat taller than (1), behind the left bloom and bending slightly toward the right.

Illustration 20

FILL A PAIR OF BUD VASES

Handsome vases — and inexpensive — are pictured in Ill. 21. But what to do with them? Have you ever flirted with Scandinavian vases like these and toyed with the idea of buying them? Have you, perhaps, succumbed? Good! Here's what to do with them:

In the forward vase place 3 sprays of fully opened freesia — (3), (4) and (5) — and 1 spray that is still in bud (6), all inclining gently to the left. Add (7), a leaf, shorter than the flowers, on the right.

Set the second vase to the left and rear of the first. In it place 2 leaves, (2), slightly taller than the flowers, and (1) considerably taller, as shown in the diagram below.

Placed on a dressing table, or on a console in an entrance hall, your simple arrangement will show to handsome advantage.

Variations? Almost any tall feathery flower will do, as will wheat stalks, palmetto fronds, tall weeds from a hayfield or even long-needled pine branches suitably trimmed. Remember, be sparing. The tall, slender leaves in back set the style for this arrangement.

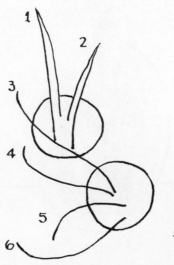

side view

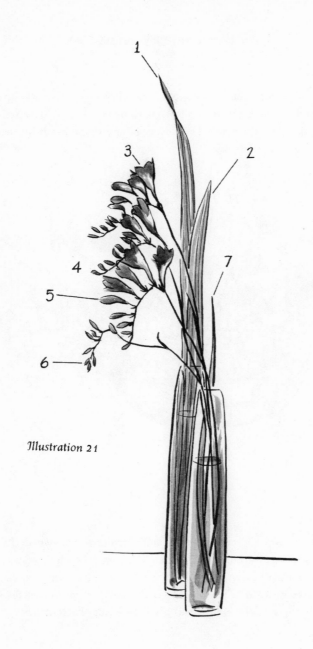

Illustration 21

99

DUCKY NURSERY NOSEGAY

It's never too soon to accustom your offspring to the gay, uplifting beauty of flowers. Of course, this Russian Khokloma lacquer duck freighted with zinnias (Ill. 22) would look lovely in any room, but it is especially appropriate in the nursery.

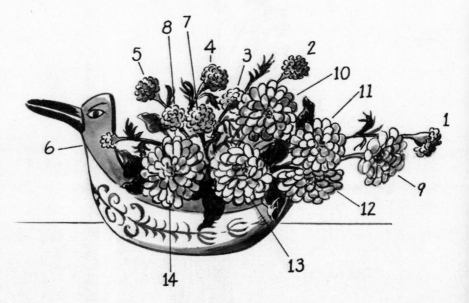

Illustration 22

Baby's silver and ceramic mugs and porringers make wonderful containers for nursery arrangements. Then if anyone asks why you're feeding baby from a plastic cup instead of the heirloom silver cup, you can say, "Baby loves to see it filled with flowers." However, to prevent the silver from tarnishing badly, set a small glass jar inside the container.

100

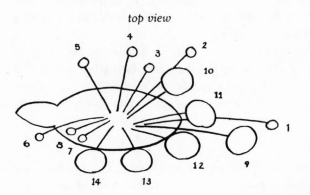

The elements for arrangement

Materials

The duck used in Ill. 22 is 5½ inches long and the colors are gold, red and green with black designs.

(1) through (6): zinnias, medium-sized, orange in color. One stalk also has a bud.

(7) through (14): deep red pompon zinnias, 1 with a bud

The schematic drawings for Ill. 22 show you the relative sizes of the flowers, and the aerial diagram shows you just where to insert each one. (1) and (9) are both slightly longer than the total length of the duck, and the others are smaller, as shown.

top view

ARRANGEMENTS COMBINED WITH SCULPTURE

One of the nicest things about flowers is the way they imbue other-wise static objects with a seeming life of their own. When you combine a statuette or any other piece of sculpture with a floral arrangement, it's hard to say which does more for the other: Does the figurine enhance the floral arrangement? Do the flowers promote the statue? It's a case of two and two adding up to more than four!

If you already own sculptured objects, Ill. 23 will give you a new insight into the role of sculpture in your home. If you have no such pieces, you will find the arrangements pleasing to look at all by themselves. But —the next time a figurine in a shop catches your eye, you will have the answer to that nagging question, "I'd love to own that, but what would I do with it?" Now you know!

Materials

(1) and (2) are torch lilies. (1) is $\frac{2}{3}$ the height of the sculpture, and (2) is $\frac{2}{3}$ the height of (1). Insert both into a frog or pin holder according to the diagram.

(3) through (5) are pairs of Spanish dagger leaves of different heights. The leaves in each pair face each other. (3) is slightly taller than the sculpture and is upright. (4) is slightly shorter and sweeps gently to the right. (5) is a bit shorter still and also bends toward the right.

The heavy pottery container shown in Ill. 23 is about 4 or 5 inches across and, as you can see, it is fairly deep for its size. A heavy crystal

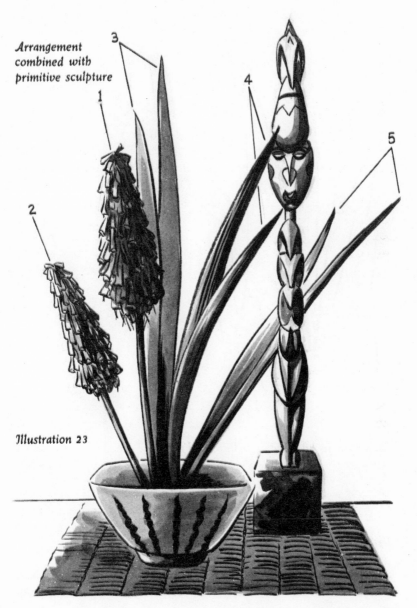

Arrangement
combined with
primitive sculpture

3

1

2

4

5

Illustration 23

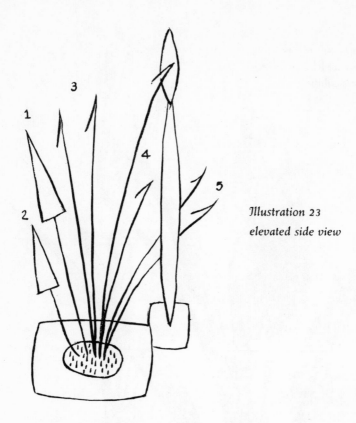

Illustration 23
elevated side view

box without its lid could serve instead of a pottery container if you have a clear glass frog rather than a pin holder. The sculpture is tall and sticklike.

Arrangement Combined with Chinese Sculpture

The harmony achieved by using a Chinese motif for sculpture, vase, mat and flowers creates a deeply satisfying arrangement. The vase may

*Arrangement combined
with Chinese
sculpture*

1

2

3

4

Illustration 24

105

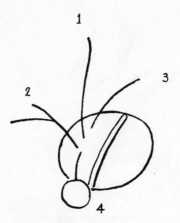

Illustration 24
top view

not be genuine Ming dynasty, but its shape and shiny plum-colored glaze give that feeling—we like to think! Vase and horse in Ill. 24 rest on a "priceless" little antique mat about 4 by 6 inches in size—possibly made by you out of a scrap of lamé from an old gown. Tarnished gold threads will give it a nice authentic look. Edge it with old velvet or satin—the more worn and used-looking the better.

Materials

Fortunately it is easy to choose flowers to go with an arrangement that is Oriental in flavor, since so many of our flowers originated in China and Japan. Here we have used one orange chrysanthemum slightly taller than the vase, with a few of its leaves left on. The two tall sprays of horse chestnuts are in the green and prickly-burr stage, while one branch contains only 3 leaves.

For a dry variation use a cluster of strawflowers to replace the chrysanthemum and either Chinese lanterns or bittersweet for the tall elements.

Arrangement Combined with Dainty Statuette

If you own a dainty, lacy statuette—Dresden or French or Meissen —chances are that you also number among your possessions an appro-

Illustration 25

priately classic container to team with it. As in all of the "idea" arrangements, the charm of your accessories determines to a large extent the successful outcome.

Our little shepherd and shepherdess combine beautifully with the fine porcelain footed bowl and the tiny roses and babies'-breath. However, any similar footed container of china, marble, alabaster, crystal, enamel, etc., would be equally satisfactory.

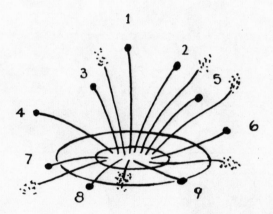

Illustration 25

top view

Materials

The flowers in Ill. 25 are sweetheart roses, some full-blown and some partly opened, with quite a few leaves left on the stems. Tea roses or even rambler roses would make good substitutes. Or you might replace the roses with miniature pink zinnias, lantana, bachelor's buttons or any suitably small flowers.

(1) through (8) : sweetheart roses
(9) through (12) : babies'-breath

SMALL ARRANGEMENTS ON A LARGE SCALE

Are you expecting 50 or 100 guests for a dessert bridge? Do you have to decorate the tables for a P.T.A. fashion show and tea? Or for a church supper? Or for any other occasion involving a great many tables? It's fun to set up an assembly line and mass-produce pretty center-pieces.

Colorful pottery custard cups make attractive containers, but you can use the glass variety if necessary. Line up as many cups as there are tables, an equal number of small pin holders, and an equal number of each item in the arrangement. The arrangement shown in Ill. 26 consists of 2 daisies, a snapdragon and 2 sprays of laurel leaves.

Materials

(1) : a large daisy. Insert it in the center, bending rearward.

(2) : a spray of laurel with 4 or 5 leaves. Insert it to the right rear.

(3) : a pink snapdragon stock. Insert it to the front, right, bending downward over the rim of the container.

(4) : spray of laurel with 2 or 3 leaves. Insert it to the left, over the rim of the cup.

(5) : small daisy. Insert it below (1), facing the front. Leave a few leaves on the daisy stem.

To achieve a smooth mass-production technique, keep your items separate. That is, put all the large daisies in one pile, the snapdragons in another, and so on. First cut all the stems as shown in the diagram accompanying Ill. 26—the tallest is about 4 inches high—and then assemble a sample arrangement. It will serve as a model for your helpers, if any!

Start your assembly line by placing a holder in each cup and half-fill the cups with water. Put all the large daisies (1) in place according

Illustration 26

top view

The five elements for each arrangement

to the above instructions. Follow up with the rest of the items, in order, and the job is done!

Variations

Springtime

(1) and (5) : daffodils
(3) : lilac
(2) and (4) : English ivy

Brilliant Red and Lavender

(1) and (5) : dark red camellias
(3) : heather
(2) and (4) : camellia leaves

Pastel

(1) and (5) : cosmos
(3) : Arrange 4 or 5 sweet pea stalks and wrap their stems together to form 1 spray.

(2) and (4) : philodendron leaves, or hosta leaves (pale white and green), arranged in clusters held with a bit of string or cellophane tape

Autumn

  (1) and (5) : yellow chrysanthemums
  (3) : spray of red dwarf maple
  (2) and (4) : chrysanthemum leaves

Fragrant and Fancy

  (1) and (5) : pale pink roses
  (3) : gardenia
  (2) and (4) : gardenia leaves

CORSAGES

Too often we tend to think of a corsage as something to wear to a Junior Prom, or for a Silver Wedding Anniversary, or a "bon voyage" gift for someone going on a cruise. But it's such fun to wear flowers, and such fun to make a simple, pretty corsage, you will probably find many opportunities to use your skill once you learn how.

A corsage for each guest adds a charming extra touch of hospitality at any type of membership-drive meeting. Or, a corsage for each new member of your club or ladies' auxiliary, makes her feel welcome and enables older members to extend overtures of friendship to the newcomers. A corsage is a gracious way of saying thank-you to paid-up members of any organization, and a simple way of identifying a group-within-a-group for any purpose whatever.

Little-girl guests at a birthday party love the grown-up feeling of wearing a corsage. Or let corsages serve as "icebreakers" at a boy-girl party. Present a corsage to each boy, and then let him pin it on the girl whose name is attached to it.

Materials

(1) through (3): daffodils, the longest about 5 inches, the others relatively shorter as indicated in Ill. 27.

(4) through (7): daffodil leaves. (4) should be the longest, (5) and (6) of about equal lengths, and (7), turning away from the ribbon, is the shortest.

Hold the flowers and leaves together with florist's wire. Then fold a 4-inch square of metallic wrapping paper around the stems. Tie with a bluish-green ribbon and fasten a small safety pin to the underneath side.

Illustration 27

Of course, you may want to substitute different colored ribbons on any corsage you make, depending on what you're wearing.

Variations

Tiger, Tiger, Burning Bright

If ever you need corsages by the hundreds, be sure to choose a time when tiger lilies are in bloom! Be sure, too, that you want the corsages for daytime use, for most lilies fold up at night. Between the lilies of the field and the daisies of the ditto, these corsages will cost you only a very little time and an infinitesimal amount for the ribbon. Yellowish ribbon would look lovely, but white or green are other possibilities.

Arrange 3 daisies around 1 lily, cut off the stems evenly and wrap in foil. Tie with a ribbon bow and attach a safety pin, or supply a florist's glass-headed pin.

Instead of a tiger lily, you can use almost any other kind of lily of approximate size, combined with either daisies (as above) or any flower of similar shape that looks well with the lily.

As you can see in Ill. 28, a few daisy leaves add a lacy touch of green to the corsage. You might want to consider, alternatively, using a sprig of mint with its fresh, spicy aroma.

Illustration 28

117

One large, fragrant peony bloom makes the most wonderful, showy corsage you can imagine, especially if you combine it with 2 pink tea roses and 1 rosebud. The finishing touch is a perky green ribbon bow, and the effect is rich indeed.

If you need a less elaborate corsage, and especially if you need to make a large number of corsages, you will find that the peony alone is quite satisfactory, without the little roses. You might want to use fairly wide ribbon for the bow, or even use crepe paper!

Instead of peonies you can also use hydrangeas, lilacs, snowballs or tulips for this corsage.

Illustration 29

One gladiolus stalk will go a long way when you use each individual blossom. For the corsage in Ill. 30 we used deep, deep red glads. The ends of three leaves back the corsage, and we added 3 sprays of lily of the valley for filler. A white ribbon bow sets this off to best advantage.

You can vary this color scheme *ad infinitum*, for gladioli come in a wide range of colors. For young girls, for example, try adding forget-me-nots to pink or coral glads.

White glads would combine beautifully with mock orange for the guests at a bridal shower. Use a few extra blooms in the corsage for the guest of honor.

For a white and lavender combination, use white glads and a few blossoms of lavender phlox. Each "head" of phlox will provide you with enough filler for one or two corsages.

Combine yellow glads with buttercups for an all-yellow corsage.

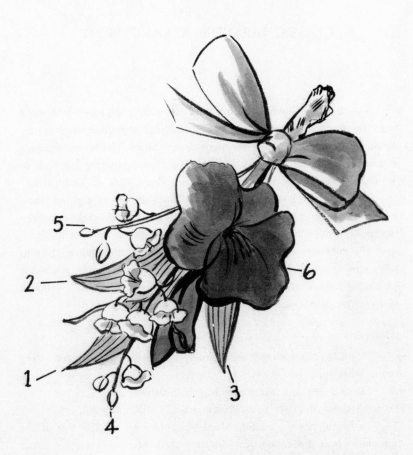

Illustration 30

CLASSIC JAPANESE ARRANGEMENT

Now that you have found out how easy—and exciting—it is to make beautiful floral arrangements, you are ready to try your hand at this *meibushi,* which is Japanese for *pièce de résistance.* The lovely grouping you admired on the jacket of the book is a classic Japanese low-style or *moribani* arrangement, designed by a professional, Mrs. F. Yoshigami.

This dramatic arrangement would enhance the top of a grand piano, a simple mantelpiece, a low corner table—in fact, it would make an arresting focal point of any part of your living room, dining room or foyer.

The container used here is free-form ceramic, unglazed on the outside, shining with a turquoise glaze inside. In its stead, you might use an oblong basket with a built-in pin holder, or, if you're lucky enough to have one, a Mexican tin tray would be most effective.

Materials

(1), (2), (5) and (6) are Japanese iris, deep purple, tinged in the center with gold.

(3) and (4) are two groups of spring daisies.

(7) through (10) : hosta leaves, one (7) still unopened.

To begin, place a medium-sized pin holder on the left side of the container. Into the center rear, insert a stalk of iris, about $1\frac{1}{2}$ times the length of the container (1).

(2) is a full-blown flower and bud $\frac{2}{3}$ the height of (1). Place it to the front left, curving slightly against (1).

(6) is another full-blown iris, slightly shorter than (1), inserted to the right and behind (1).

(5) is half the height of (6), placed to its right.

(3) is made up of four spring daisies, the tallest slightly shorter than (5). Arrange the group of four in steps, sweeping from right for the tallest to front left for the shortest.

122

Illustration 31

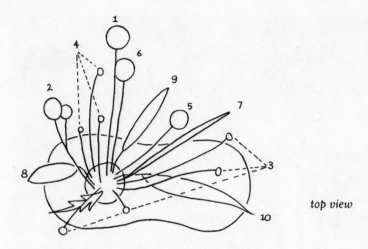

top view

(4) is another group of three daisies, placed in the rear between (1) and (2).

(7) : thin, unopened hosta leaf inserted in line with daisies in the foreground.

(8) : full hosta leaf, to the left and rear of (1), bending sharply down.

(9) : another opened hosta leaf, inserted at the back of the arrangement, between (6) and (5), bending to the back.

(10) : the last glossy leaf, inserted at the right to sweep low across the rim of the container.

This striking arrangement is particularly attractive against a light, otherwise unadorned background.

Variation

In place of the vivid purple irises, you might try exotic speckled tiger lilies, with ruby-red pompons replacing the golden daisies. Reddish-brown plantain lily leaves would add just the right note of intensity against a dark wall. Try this in a terra cotta casserole.

124